CLIMATE CRISIS

100 Stories from the Frontline

Geoffrey Zachary

CONTENTS

GEOFFREYZACHARY

Climate Crisis:
100 Stories from the Frontlines

PART I: UNDERSTANDING THE CLIMATE CRISIS

CHAPTER 1: INTRODUCTION TO THE CLIMATE CRISIS

Introduction:
The climate crisis is one of the most pressing issues of our time, posing significant threats to our planet and its inhabitants. In this chapter, we will explore the fundamental aspects of the climate crisis, including its causes, impacts, and the urgent need for action.

Understanding the Climate Crisis:
The climate crisis refers to the long-term changes in Earth's climate patterns, primarily attributed to human activities, such as the burning of fossil fuels and deforestation. The increase in greenhouse gas emissions, particularly carbon dioxide, traps heat in the atmosphere, leading to a rise in global temperatures and disrupting natural ecosystems.

Causes of the Climate Crisis:
Human activities, such as the burning of fossil fuels for energy production, transportation, and industrial processes, are the primary contributors to the climate crisis. Deforestation, which reduces the Earth's capacity to absorb carbon dioxide, is another significant factor. The release of greenhouse gases into the atmosphere intensifies the greenhouse effect, causing global warming.

Impacts of the Climate Crisis:

The climate crisis has far-reaching impacts on various aspects of our lives and the environment. Rising temperatures lead to more frequent and severe heatwaves, droughts, and wildfires. Melting ice caps and glaciers contribute to sea-level rise, threatening coastal communities. Extreme weather events, including hurricanes and floods, are becoming more frequent and intense. Changes in precipitation patterns affect agriculture and food security.

Real-Life Examples:
One prominent real-life example of the climate crisis is the melting of the polar ice caps in the Arctic. The reduction in ice coverage not only affects wildlife and their habitats but also contributes to rising sea levels. This poses a significant threat to low-lying islands and coastal cities, where communities are already experiencing the impacts of increased flooding and erosion.

Another example is the increased frequency and intensity of wildfires around the world. In recent years, regions like California, Australia, and the Amazon rainforest have witnessed devastating fires, causing loss of life, destruction of ecosystems, and releasing massive amounts of carbon dioxide into the atmosphere.

The Need for Urgent Action:
The consequences of the climate crisis are already being felt, and the window of opportunity to prevent further damage is narrowing. Urgent action is necessary to reduce greenhouse gas emissions, transition to renewable energy sources, conserve natural resources and adapt to a changing climate. Governments, businesses, and individuals all have a role to play in addressing the climate crisis and ensuring a sustainable future for generations to come.

Conclusion:
The introduction to the climate crisis sets the stage for understanding the gravity of the situation we face. The evidence

of climate change is undeniable, and the need for action is urgent. In the subsequent chapters of this book, we will delve deeper into various aspects of the climate crisis, exploring the impacts on different sectors, the role of policy and innovation, and the inspiring stories of individuals and communities working towards a sustainable future. Together, we can tackle the climate crisis and create a resilient and environmentally conscious world.

CHAPTER 2: THE SCIENCE OF CLIMATE CHANGE

Introduction:
In this chapter, we will delve into the scientific foundations of climate change, exploring the mechanisms and evidence that support our understanding of this global crisis. Understanding science is crucial for grasping the urgency of the situation and the need for collective action.

The Greenhouse Effect:
The greenhouse effect is a natural process by which certain gases in the Earth's atmosphere trap heat from the sun, keeping the planet warm and habitable. However, human activities, such as the burning of fossil fuels and deforestation, have increased the concentration of greenhouse gases, leading to an enhanced greenhouse effect and global warming.

The Role of Greenhouse Gases:
Carbon dioxide (CO_2) is the primary greenhouse gas responsible for climate change. Other greenhouse gases, such as methane (CH_4) and nitrous oxide (N_2O), also contribute to the warming effect. Human activities, including the burning of fossil fuels, deforestation, and agricultural practices, have significantly increased the levels of these gases in the atmosphere.

Temperature Records and Climate Models:
Scientists have analysed temperature records from around the

world and used sophisticated climate models to project future changes. These models simulate the Earth's climate system based on various factors, including greenhouse gas emissions, solar radiation, and atmospheric conditions. The consensus among climate scientists is that human activities are the primary driver of the observed warming trends.

Real-Life Examples:
One compelling real-life example of the science behind climate change is the study of ice cores. Scientists drill deep into glaciers and ice sheets to extract ice cores that contain trapped air bubbles. By analysing the composition of these air bubbles, researchers can reconstruct past atmospheric conditions and determine historic levels of greenhouse gases. This evidence confirms the correlation between greenhouse gas concentrations and global temperatures.

Another example is the observation of melting glaciers and ice caps worldwide. Glaciers act as natural indicators of climate change, as their retreat is a visible consequence of rising temperatures. The retreat of glaciers threatens water supplies for communities that rely on them for freshwater sources, impacting agriculture, hydropower, and ecosystem stability.

Impacts of Climate Change:
The science of climate change also reveals the wide-ranging impacts on ecosystems, weather patterns, and human societies. Rising temperatures lead to more frequent and intense heat waves, altering the distribution of plant and animal species and disrupting ecosystems. Changes in precipitation patterns result in more severe droughts and floods, affecting agriculture, water availability, and biodiversity. Rising sea levels threaten coastal communities and exacerbate the damage caused by storms and erosion.

Conclusion:
Understanding the science of climate change is essential for recognizing its causes, impacts, and potential solutions. The

scientific consensus leaves no doubt that human activities are driving the unprecedented changes in our climate system. Real-life examples and observations provide tangible evidence of the science at work. By recognizing the role, we play in climate change, we can take collective action to mitigate its effects, transition to cleaner energy sources, and build a sustainable future for ourselves and future generations. In the following chapters, we will explore the social, economic, and policy aspects of the climate crisis, shedding light on inspiring stories of resilience and innovation in the face of this global challenge.

CHAPTER 3: THE HISTORY AND CAUSES OF THE CLIMATE CRISIS

Introduction:
In this chapter, we will delve into the historical context and underlying causes that have led to the current climate crisis. Understanding the roots of the problem is crucial for developing effective solutions and addressing the challenges we face today.

The Historical Context:
The Earth's climate has experienced natural fluctuations throughout its history, driven by factors such as volcanic activity, variations in solar radiation, and changes in the Earth's orbit. However, the current climate crisis is unprecedented and primarily caused by human activities over the past few centuries.

Industrial Revolution and Fossil Fuels:
The Industrial Revolution, which began in the 18th century, marked a turning point in human history. It brought about significant advancements in technology and economic development but also introduced a heavy reliance on fossil fuels, such as coal, oil, and natural gas. The combustion of these fuels releases carbon dioxide (CO_2) and other greenhouse gases into the atmosphere, contributing to global warming.

Deforestation and Land Use Change:
The clearing of forests, primarily for agriculture, logging, and urbanization, has significantly contributed to the climate crisis. Forests act as carbon sinks, absorbing CO2 from the atmosphere. Deforestation disrupts this process, releasing stored carbon and reducing the Earth's capacity to mitigate climate change. Additionally, deforestation reduces biodiversity and alters regional climate patterns.

Population Growth and Consumption:
The exponential growth of the global population and increasing levels of consumption have placed immense pressure on the Earth's resources and ecosystems. As more people strive for improved living standards, the demand for energy, food, and goods has soared. This demand, coupled with inefficient production and consumption practices, has intensified the emission of greenhouse gases and environmental degradation.

Real-Life Examples:
One significant historical example of human-induced climate change is the rise of carbon dioxide levels in the atmosphere. Scientists have been able to measure atmospheric CO2 concentrations using ice cores and other methods, revealing a sharp increase since the Industrial Revolution. This direct correlation between CO2 emissions and human activities demonstrates our role in the current climate crisis.

Another example is the acceleration of deforestation in the Amazon rainforest. The Amazon, known as the "lungs of the Earth," plays a critical role in regulating global climate patterns. However, deforestation driven by agriculture and illegal logging threatens the region's ability to sequester carbon and disrupts the water cycle, contributing to climate change.

The Role of Policy and International Agreements:
International efforts to address the climate crisis have gained momentum over the years. The United Nations Framework

Convention on Climate Change (UNFCCC) was established in 1992, with subsequent agreements like the Kyoto Protocol and the Paris Agreement aiming to mitigate greenhouse gas emissions and support sustainable development. These agreements highlight the importance of global cooperation in tackling the climate crisis.

Conclusion:

The history and causes of the climate crisis reveal the interplay between human activities, economic development, and environmental degradation. The reliance on fossil fuels, deforestation, population growth, and consumption patterns have significantly contributed to the current climate crisis. Real-life examples demonstrate the tangible impacts of these factors on the environment and society.

Addressing the climate crisis requires a multifaceted approach that combines policy interventions, technological advancements, and individual actions. By understanding the historical context and causes of the crisis, we can collectively work towards sustainable solutions and a more resilient future. In the following chapters, we will explore the consequences of climate change, innovative strategies for mitigation and adaptation, and the crucial role of individuals, communities, and governments in shaping a sustainable and climate-resilient world.

CHAPTER 4: IMPACTS OF CLIMATE CHANGE ON THE ENVIRONMENT

Introduction:
In this chapter, we will explore the wide-ranging impacts of climate change on the environment. The consequences of global warming and related climate phenomena have far-reaching effects on ecosystems, biodiversity, natural resources, and overall planetary health.

1. Rising Temperatures:
One of the most evident impacts of climate change is the increase in global temperatures. Rising temperatures have numerous consequences, including the melting of glaciers and polar ice caps. This leads to rising sea levels, endangering coastal communities and ecosystems. Real-life examples include the rapid retreat of glaciers such as those in the Arctic and the Antarctic, contributing to sea-level rise and disrupting delicate ecosystems.

2. Changes in Precipitation Patterns:
Climate change also influences precipitation patterns, resulting in more frequent and intense weather events, including droughts and heavy rainfall. These shifts have severe implications for agriculture, water availability, and biodiversity. For instance, prolonged droughts can lead to reduced crop yields, water

scarcity, and increased wildfire risks, as experienced in regions like California, Australia, and parts of Africa.

3. Ecosystem Disruption:

Climate change disrupts ecosystems by altering the timing of seasonal events and affecting species' habitats and migration patterns. Many plant and animal species are struggling to adapt to rapidly changing environmental conditions, leading to shifts in their geographical ranges and potential extinction risks. The bleaching of coral reefs, driven by warmer ocean temperatures, is an alarming example of how climate change devastates sensitive marine ecosystems.

4. Loss of Biodiversity:

The loss of biodiversity is a significant consequence of climate change. Species unable to adapt to changing conditions may face reduced populations or even extinction. The decline of iconic species like polar bears, whose habitat is melting away due to shrinking sea ice, exemplifies the devastating impact of climate change on vulnerable wildlife populations.

5. Disruption of Natural Cycles:

Climate change disrupts natural cycles that maintain the balance of ecosystems. For instance, the timing of flowering and pollination may become out of sync, affecting plant reproduction and the survival of pollinators like bees and butterflies. This disruption can have cascading effects throughout the food web, ultimately impacting human food security.

6. Ocean Acidification:

Increasing carbon dioxide levels in the atmosphere lead to ocean acidification, as the oceans absorb a significant portion of the excess CO_2. This acidification poses a threat to marine organisms with calcium carbonate shells, such as shellfish and coral reefs, as it inhibits their ability to build and maintain their protective structures. The decline of shellfish populations and the deterioration of coral reefs are tangible outcomes of ocean acidification.

Conclusion:
The impacts of climate change on the environment are vast and multifaceted. Rising temperatures, changes in precipitation patterns, ecosystem disruption, loss of biodiversity, disruption of natural cycles, and ocean acidification are just some of the consequences we face. Real-life examples highlight the urgency of addressing climate change and adopting sustainable practices to mitigate its effects.

Understanding the impacts of climate change on the environment is crucial for developing effective strategies for adaptation and mitigation. By conserving natural habitats, reducing greenhouse gas emissions, and promoting sustainable land and resource management, we can work towards safeguarding the environment and preserving Earth's ecological balance. In the following chapters, we will explore the social and economic impacts of climate change, examine strategies for resilience and adaptation, and discuss the role of individuals and communities in combating the climate crisis.

PART II: VOICES FROM THE FRONTLINES

CHAPTER 5: THE INDIGENOUS COMMUNITIES AND CLIMATE CHANGE

Introduction:
In this chapter, we delve into the significant relationship between indigenous communities and climate change. Indigenous peoples have a deep connection to the land, relying on traditional knowledge and sustainable practices that have sustained their communities for centuries. However, they are among the most vulnerable to the impacts of climate change, with their livelihoods, cultures, and identities at stake.

1. Indigenous Knowledge and Climate Adaptation:
Indigenous communities possess invaluable traditional knowledge and practices that can contribute to climate adaptation strategies. Their observations of subtle changes in weather patterns, ecosystems, and animal behaviour over generations provide unique insights into the impacts of climate change. For example, in the Arctic, Inuit communities have observed the thinning and cracking of sea ice, affecting their hunting and fishing practices. Incorporating indigenous knowledge into climate change research and policy can enhance resilience and adaptation efforts.

2. Land-based Livelihoods:

Indigenous peoples often rely on land-based livelihoods, such as agriculture, fishing, hunting, and gathering. However, climate change disrupts these activities by altering ecosystems, diminishing resources, and introducing new challenges. For instance, indigenous communities in the Amazon rainforest face deforestation, changing rainfall patterns, and increased risks of wildfires, impacting their ability to sustain themselves. These communities often face the loss of traditional practices and the need to adapt to new economic and social circumstances.

3. Cultural Impacts:

Climate change also poses cultural threats to indigenous communities. The destruction of natural habitats and the loss of biodiversity undermine traditional spiritual practices, ceremonies, and cultural identities tied to the land. Real-life examples include the displacement of indigenous communities due to rising sea levels in low-lying coastal regions, forcing them to abandon ancestral lands and disrupting their cultural practices.

4. Environmental Stewardship:

Indigenous communities have long served as stewards of the environment, practising sustainable land and resource management that preserves biodiversity and ecosystems. Their traditional practices, such as rotational farming and forest conservation, contribute to climate change mitigation by sequestering carbon and protecting natural carbon sinks. These practices can offer valuable lessons for sustainable resource management and climate action worldwide.

5. Advocacy and Resilience:

Indigenous communities are increasingly at the forefront of climate activism and resilience-building efforts. They advocate for their rights, land sovereignty, and the recognition of traditional knowledge in climate policies. The Standing Rock protests in the United States against the Dakota Access Pipeline and the activism of the Sami people in Scandinavia are powerful examples of indigenous communities standing up for environmental justice and climate action.

Conclusion:
Indigenous communities play a crucial role in understanding and addressing the challenges posed by climate change. Their traditional knowledge, land-based livelihoods, cultural resilience, and environmental stewardship offer valuable insights and solutions. It is essential to prioritize the inclusion of indigenous perspectives and support their rights and self-determination in climate change policies and actions.

Collaboration and partnership with indigenous communities are essential to achieving sustainable and equitable solutions to the climate crisis. By recognizing and respecting the knowledge and experiences of indigenous peoples, we can foster resilience, protect cultural heritage, and work towards a more sustainable future for all. In the next chapters, we will explore the role of governments, organizations, and individuals in supporting indigenous communities and advancing climate justice.

CHAPTER 6: FARMERS AND AGRICULTURAL WORKERS BATTLING CLIMATE CHANGE

Introduction:
In this chapter, we explore the crucial role of farmers and agricultural workers in confronting the challenges posed by climate change. Agriculture is inherently dependent on climate and weather patterns, making it highly vulnerable to the impacts of a changing climate. However, farmers are also at the forefront of implementing innovative strategies to mitigate and adapt to these changes, ensuring food security and sustainable agricultural practices.

1. Climate Change and Agricultural Challenges:
Climate change presents numerous challenges for farmers, including shifting weather patterns, increased frequency of extreme weather events, and changing pest and disease dynamics. These factors disrupt traditional farming practices and threaten crop yields and livestock production. For example, prolonged droughts in regions like California and Australia have reduced water availability for irrigation, affecting crop productivity and leading to economic losses for farmers.

2. Innovative Farming Practices:
Farmers are adopting innovative techniques and practices to

mitigate and adapt to climate change. These include precision agriculture, agroforestry, conservation agriculture, and the use of climate-resilient crop varieties. Precision agriculture uses technology and data to optimize resource use, such as water and fertilizers, minimizing environmental impact. Agroforestry combines trees with crops, enhancing biodiversity, improving soil health, and sequestering carbon. Conservation agriculture focuses on reducing soil erosion and improving soil health through minimal tillage, crop rotation, and cover cropping.

3. Sustainable Water Management:
Water scarcity is a significant concern in agriculture, exacerbated by climate change. Farmers are implementing sustainable water management practices to cope with this challenge. This includes drip irrigation, rainwater harvesting, and the use of efficient irrigation systems. For instance, in regions facing water scarcity, such as parts of India, farmers have adopted drip irrigation techniques, reduced water usage while maintaining crop productivity.

4. Climate-Smart Agriculture:
Climate-smart agriculture integrates adaptation, mitigation, and productivity goals, addressing the interconnections between agriculture and climate change. It aims to build resilience, reduce greenhouse gas emissions, and increase food security. Real-life examples of climate-smart agriculture initiatives include the System of Rice Intensification (SRI), which promotes water-efficient rice cultivation, and the promotion of agroecological practices that enhance biodiversity and soil health.

5. Farmer-Led Initiatives and Knowledge Sharing:
Farmers play a vital role in sharing knowledge, experiences, and innovations to address climate change. Farmer-led initiatives, such as farmer field schools, cooperative networks, and participatory research, facilitate the exchange of best practices and foster collective action. For example, farmer field schools in sub-Saharan Africa have empowered farmers to adopt climate-

smart techniques and adapt to changing conditions.

6. Government Support and Policy:
Government policies and support are critical in enabling farmers to tackle climate change effectively. This includes providing incentives for climate-smart practices, supporting research and development, and ensuring access to affordable and climate-resilient technologies. Collaborative efforts between governments, agricultural organizations, and farmers' associations are essential to driving sustainable agricultural practices.

Conclusion:
Farmers and agricultural workers are on the frontlines of climate change, facing numerous challenges to ensure food security and sustainable farming practices. Their resilience, innovation, and adoption of climate-smart strategies are crucial for building a more resilient and sustainable agricultural sector. Supporting farmers with access to knowledge, technology, and policy frameworks that prioritize climate change adaptation and mitigation is essential for securing food production and achieving global climate goals.

The examples and practices highlighted in this chapter demonstrate the potential for agriculture to contribute to climate change solutions. By working together and supporting farmers, we can create a more resilient and sustainable agricultural system that addresses the challenges of a changing climate and ensures food security for present and future generations.

CHAPTER 7: COASTAL COMMUNITIES AND RISING SEA LEVELS

Introduction:
In this chapter, we explore the impacts of rising sea levels on coastal communities and the efforts undertaken to adapt to these challenges. With climate change causing the melting of ice caps and thermal expansion of seawater, sea levels are rising at an accelerated rate. This poses significant threats to coastal areas, including increased flooding, erosion, and saltwater intrusion. Coastal communities are at the forefront of dealing with these consequences and implementing strategies to mitigate the risks.

1. Impacts of Rising Sea Levels:
Rising sea levels have profound impacts on coastal communities. Low-lying areas are particularly vulnerable, experiencing more frequent and severe coastal flooding. This leads to property damage, loss of infrastructure, and displacement of populations. Coastal erosion accelerates as sea levels rise, endangering homes, beaches, and ecosystems. Furthermore, saltwater intrusion contaminates freshwater sources, affecting agriculture and drinking water supplies.

2. Coastal Adaptation Strategies:
Coastal communities are implementing a range of adaptation strategies to cope with rising sea levels. These include coastal defence systems such as seawalls, dikes, and flood barriers, which

protect against storm surges and flooding. Nature-based solutions like wetland restoration and beach nourishment help absorb wave energy and enhance shoreline resilience. Managed retreat, the strategic relocation of vulnerable communities away from the coastline, is also being considered in some cases.

3. Integrated Coastal Zone Management:
Integrated Coastal Zone Management (ICZM) approaches aim to balance environmental, social, and economic considerations to sustainably manage coastal areas. These strategies involve collaboration between stakeholders, including governments, local communities, and businesses. ICZM frameworks facilitate the coordination of coastal development, land use planning, and natural resource management to ensure the long-term resilience of coastal communities.

4. Community Engagement and Empowerment:
Coastal communities are actively engaging in decision-making processes and community-driven initiatives to address the impacts of rising sea levels. Examples include participatory mapping exercises to identify vulnerable areas, community-based monitoring of sea level rise, and grassroots organizations advocating for climate-resilient practices. These efforts foster community empowerment, knowledge sharing, and collective action.

5. Real-Life Examples of Coastal Adaptation:
Several coastal communities around the world are implementing innovative adaptation strategies. For instance, the city of Rotterdam in the Netherlands has adopted a multifaceted approach to managing sea level rise, combining innovative architectural designs, water storage systems, and floating infrastructure. The Maldives, a low-lying island nation, is exploring the use of artificial reefs and mangrove restoration to reduce coastal erosion and protect against storm surges.

6. International Cooperation and Funding:

Addressing the challenges of rising sea levels requires international cooperation and financial support. Global initiatives like the United Nations Framework Convention on Climate Change (UNFCCC) and the Green Climate Fund aim to assist developing countries in adapting to climate change impacts. International partnerships and funding mechanisms facilitate the sharing of knowledge, technology, and resources to support coastal adaptation efforts.

Conclusion:
Coastal communities face significant challenges from rising sea levels, including increased flooding, erosion, and saltwater intrusion. However, through the implementation of adaptation strategies, community engagement, and international cooperation, these communities are finding innovative solutions to protect their homes and livelihoods. The examples highlighted in this chapter demonstrate that coastal adaptation is possible with a combination of infrastructure development, nature-based solutions, and community empowerment. By working together and supporting coastal communities, we can build resilience and safeguard vulnerable areas from the impacts of rising sea levels, ensuring a sustainable future for coastal regions and the people who call them home.

CHAPTER 8: URBAN AREAS AND THE HEAT ISLAND EFFECT

Introduction:

In this chapter, we delve into the challenges that urban areas face with the heat island effect and the strategies employed to mitigate its impacts. As cities continue to grow and urbanize, they face unique climate-related challenges, with the heat island effect being one of the most significant. The heat island effect refers to the phenomenon where urban areas experience higher temperatures than surrounding rural areas due to human activities and the built environment. This chapter explores the impacts of the heat island effect, discusses its causes, and examines strategies that cities are implementing to combat it.

1. The Heat Island Effect:

The heat island effect occurs when urban areas, characterized by the abundance of buildings, pavement, and infrastructure, absorb, and re-emit heat, leading to elevated temperatures. This effect is exacerbated by factors such as reduced vegetation, increased energy consumption, and altered airflow patterns. The result is higher temperatures in urban areas compared to nearby rural regions, particularly during heatwaves and summer months.

2. Impacts on Urban Areas:

The heat island effect poses significant challenges for urban areas.

Higher temperatures can have adverse effects on human health, increasing the risk of heat-related illnesses and even mortality. Additionally, the increased demand for cooling during hot periods puts a strain on energy infrastructure, leading to higher energy consumption and greenhouse gas emissions. The heat island effect also impacts urban ecosystems, altering microclimates and contributing to the loss of biodiversity.

3. Causes of the Heat Island Effect:
The heat island effect is primarily caused by human activities and urban infrastructure. Factors such as the extensive use of asphalt and concrete, lack of green spaces, and the concentration of heat-absorbing buildings contribute to elevated temperatures. Other factors include waste heat from industrial and commercial activities, vehicular emissions, and the limited penetration of natural cooling mechanisms.

4. Mitigation Strategies:
Cities are implementing various strategies to mitigate the heat island effect and create more liveable urban environments. These include:

a. Increasing Green Spaces: Planting trees, creating parks, and incorporating green roofs and walls help to enhance urban vegetation and provide shade, reducing surface temperatures and cooling the surrounding air.

b. Cool Roofs and Pavements: Using reflective materials for roofs and pavements can reduce heat absorption, limiting temperature increases and lowering energy demand for cooling.

c. Urban Design and Planning: Implementing urban design strategies that prioritize natural ventilation, pedestrian-friendly environments, and mixed land use can promote airflow and reduce the heat island effect.

d. Water Features: Incorporating water bodies, fountains, and misting systems can help cool urban areas through evaporation and create a pleasant microclimate.

e. Sustainable Building Practices: Adopting energy-efficient building designs, such as green buildings and passive cooling techniques, can minimize heat generation and reduce the need for artificial cooling.

f. Community Engagement and Education: Raising awareness and engaging the community in heat island mitigation efforts can lead to more sustainable behaviours and practices.

5. Real-Life Examples:
Numerous cities worldwide have implemented heat island mitigation strategies with positive outcomes. For instance, Singapore has launched the "Cooling Singapore" initiative, which includes measures such as increasing green spaces, constructing cool corridors, and implementing cool roofs and facades. The city of Los Angeles in the United States has implemented the "Cool Streets LA" program, which involves coating streets with a reflective material to reduce surface temperatures and improve comfort for pedestrians.

Conclusion:
The heat island effect poses significant challenges for urban areas, affecting human health, energy consumption, and urban ecosystems. However, through the implementation of mitigation strategies such as increasing green spaces, adopting cool roofs and pavements, and promoting sustainable urban design, cities can effectively combat the heat island effect. Real-life examples demonstrate that proactive measures can significantly improve urban liveability and reduce the environmental impacts associated with higher temperatures. By prioritizing sustainable urban planning and engaging communities, cities can create more resilient and comfortable environments for their residents while mitigating the adverse effects of the heat island effect.

PART III: SOLUTIONS AND INNOVATIONS

CHAPTER 9: RENEWABLE ENERGY AND THE TRANSITION TO A LOW-CARBON FUTURE

Introduction:

In this chapter, we explore the role of renewable energy in combating climate change and transitioning to a low-carbon future. As the world grapples with the impacts of climate change, the need to reduce greenhouse gas emissions and shift towards cleaner energy sources becomes increasingly urgent. Renewable energy, derived from sources such as solar, wind, hydro, and geothermal, offers a sustainable alternative to fossil fuels. This chapter examines the benefits of renewable energy, explores its current usage and potential, and discusses the challenges and opportunities in the transition to a low-carbon future.

1. The Benefits of Renewable Energy:

Renewable energy sources have numerous advantages over fossil fuels. They are clean, emitting little to no greenhouse gases during operation, thereby mitigating climate change. They are also abundant and widely distributed, offering the potential for energy independence and security. Additionally, renewable energy can stimulate economic growth, create jobs, and improve energy access in rural and remote areas.

2. Current Usage and Potential of Renewable Energy:
Renewable energy has experienced significant growth in recent years. Solar and wind power have become increasingly cost-effective, leading to the rapid deployment of solar panels and wind turbines worldwide. Hydroelectric power remains the largest source of renewable energy, while geothermal and biomass also contribute to the renewable energy mix. The potential for renewable energy is vast, with studies showing that it could meet a significant portion of global energy demand.

3. Challenges and Opportunities in the Transition to Renewable Energy:
While renewable energy offers many benefits, there are challenges to its widespread adoption. The intermittent nature of some renewable sources, such as solar and wind, require innovative solutions for energy storage and grid integration. The upfront costs of renewable energy technologies can also be a barrier, although prices have been decreasing. The transition to renewable energy requires supportive policies, investment in infrastructure, and public awareness and acceptance.

4. Real-Life Examples:
Numerous real-life examples showcase the successful integration of renewable energy into the energy mix. Germany, for instance, has made significant progress in transitioning to renewable energy through its Energiewende (Energy Transition) initiative. The country has increased its share of renewable energy, with solar and wind power accounting for a substantial portion of its electricity generation. Costa Rica has achieved nearly 100% renewable electricity generation, primarily from hydro, wind, and geothermal sources. The state of California in the United States has set ambitious renewable energy goals and has become a leader in solar energy adoption.

5. Supporting the Transition:

To accelerate the transition to renewable energy, governments, businesses, and individuals must take action. This includes:

a. Policy Support: Governments can establish supportive policies such as feed-in tariffs, tax incentives, and renewable energy targets to encourage investment and adoption of renewable energy technologies.

b. Investment and Research: Increased investment in renewable energy infrastructure, research and development, and innovation can drive technological advancements and cost reductions.

c. Public Awareness and Education: Educating the public about the benefits of renewable energy and the urgency of addressing climate change can foster support and drive demand for clean energy solutions.

d. Collaboration and Partnerships: Collaboration between governments, businesses, and communities is crucial to overcoming challenges and fostering a collective effort in the transition to renewable energy.

e. Energy Efficiency: Improving energy efficiency in all sectors, including buildings, transportation, and industry, can reduce overall energy demand and complement the integration of renewable energy.

Conclusion:
Renewable energy holds immense potential in addressing the challenges of climate change and transitioning to a low-carbon future. Its benefits, including reduced greenhouse gas emissions, job creation, and energy security, make it a crucial component of global efforts to combat climate change. Real-life examples demonstrate that the transition to renewable energy is not only feasible but also economically and environmentally advantageous. By supporting policies, investment, research, and public awareness, we can accelerate the adoption of renewable energy and pave the way for a sustainable and low-carbon future.

CHAPTER 10: SUSTAINABLE TRANSPORTATION AND REDUCING EMISSIONS

Introduction:
Transportation is a significant contributor to greenhouse gas emissions, making it a crucial sector to address in the fight against climate change. In this chapter, we explore the challenges posed by transportation-related emissions and the solutions available to create a more sustainable transportation system. We examine the role of electric vehicles, public transportation, alternative fuels, and innovative transportation initiatives in reducing emissions and building a greener future.

1. The Environmental Impact of Transportation:
Transportation accounts for a significant portion of global greenhouse gas emissions, primarily due to the combustion of fossil fuels in vehicles. The emissions from cars, trucks, ships, aeroplanes, and trains contribute to air pollution, climate change, and negative health effects. It is essential to transition to sustainable transportation systems that reduce reliance on fossil fuels and minimize environmental impact.

2. Electric Vehicles (EVs):

Electric vehicles are a promising solution for reducing emissions in the transportation sector. They produce zero tailpipe emissions and have significantly lower lifecycle emissions compared to traditional internal combustion engine vehicles. Advances in battery technology, charging infrastructure, and government incentives have facilitated the growth of the electric vehicle market. Real-life examples, such as Norway's success in promoting EV adoption and companies transitioning their fleet to electric vehicles, demonstrate the positive impact of EVs.

3. Public Transportation:
Efficient and accessible public transportation plays a vital role in reducing emissions by providing an alternative to individual car usage. Well-designed public transportation systems, including buses, trains, and light rail, can significantly reduce traffic congestion and decrease emissions. Real-life examples, such as the comprehensive public transportation systems in cities like Tokyo and Zurich, showcase the benefits of investing in sustainable mass transit.

4. Alternative Fuels:
Another strategy to reduce transportation emissions is the use of alternative fuels. Biofuels, such as ethanol and biodiesel, offer lower carbon intensity compared to fossil fuels and can be blended with traditional gasoline and diesel. Hydrogen fuel cells are another option, providing zero-emission transportation when produced from renewable sources. Real-life examples include Brazil's extensive use of ethanol in its vehicle fleet and the growing adoption of hydrogen fuel cell vehicles in countries like Japan and South Korea.

5. Innovative Transportation Initiatives:
Innovative transportation initiatives, including ridesharing, carpooling, bike-sharing, and pedestrian-friendly urban planning, contribute to reducing emissions and promoting sustainable transportation options. For example, cities like Amsterdam and Copenhagen have prioritized cycling

infrastructure, leading to a significant modal shift from cars to bicycles. Ridesharing platforms like Uber and Lyft have also contributed to reducing vehicle miles travelled and emissions in urban areas.

6. Government Policies and Support:
Government policies play a crucial role in promoting sustainable transportation practices. These may include incentives for electric vehicles, funding for public transportation infrastructure, and regulations on vehicle emissions. Real-life examples, such as California's Zero Emission Vehicle (ZEV) mandate and the European Union's stricter emission standards for automobiles, highlight the importance of policy support in driving the transition to sustainable transportation.

Conclusion:
Sustainable transportation is a key component of mitigating climate change and reducing emissions. By transitioning to electric vehicles, expanding, and improving public transportation systems, promoting alternative fuels, and implementing innovative transportation initiatives, we can create a more sustainable and environmentally friendly transportation sector. Real-life examples demonstrate that sustainable transportation solutions are both feasible and beneficial, reducing emissions, improving air quality, and enhancing the overall quality of life in communities. Government policies and public support are crucial in accelerating the adoption of sustainable transportation practices and building a greener future for generations to come.

CHAPTER 11: GREEN BUILDINGS AND ENERGY EFFICIENCY

Introduction:
In the face of climate change, the construction and operation of buildings play a significant role in energy consumption and greenhouse gas emissions. Green buildings and energy-efficient practices offer solutions to reduce the environmental impact of the built environment. In this chapter, we explore the importance of green buildings, the principles of energy efficiency, and real-life examples of sustainable building practices that contribute to climate change mitigation.

1. The Environmental Impact of Buildings:
Buildings account for a substantial portion of global energy use and greenhouse gas emissions. The construction, operation, and maintenance of buildings consume vast amounts of energy, primarily from non-renewable sources. As the world population grows and urbanization continues, the demand for buildings increases, making it crucial to adopt sustainable practices that minimize energy consumption and reduce carbon emissions.

2. Green Building Principles:
Green buildings are designed and constructed to minimize their environmental impact while maximizing energy efficiency, water efficiency, and occupant comfort. Key principles of green buildings include energy-efficient design, use of

renewable materials, water conservation, waste reduction, and indoor environmental quality. These principles guide architects, builders, and developers in creating environmentally responsible and resource-efficient structures.

3. Energy Efficiency in Buildings:
Energy efficiency is a crucial aspect of green buildings and involves optimizing the use of energy to reduce waste and minimize greenhouse gas emissions. It encompasses various measures such as efficient heating, ventilation, and air conditioning (HVAC) systems, insulation, lighting controls, and energy-efficient appliances. Real-life examples, such as LEED-certified buildings and net-zero energy buildings, showcase the successful implementation of energy-efficient practices.

4. Sustainable Materials and Construction:
The selection of sustainable materials and construction practices is essential for reducing the environmental impact of buildings. This includes using recycled or renewable materials, reducing waste during construction, and implementing green building certifications. Examples of sustainable materials include bamboo, reclaimed wood, recycled steel, and low-emission paints. Adopting sustainable construction practices can significantly reduce the carbon footprint of buildings.

5. Net-Zero Energy Buildings:
Net-zero energy buildings generate as much energy as they consume over a defined period, typically a year. They achieve this through a combination of energy-efficient design, on-site renewable energy generation, and energy storage. Net-zero energy buildings not only minimize their environmental impact but also provide a pathway towards a carbon-neutral future. Real-life examples, such as the Bullitt Centre in Seattle and the PNC Tower in Pittsburgh, demonstrate the feasibility and benefits of net-zero energy buildings.

6. Government Policies and Incentives:

Government policies and incentives play a crucial role in promoting the adoption of green building practices and energy efficiency. These may include building codes, energy performance standards, financial incentives, and tax benefits. For instance, the Leadership in Energy and Environmental Design (LEED) certification program provides recognition and incentives for sustainable building practices. Real-life examples of successful government policies, such as California's Title 24 building energy efficiency standards, showcase the positive impact of regulatory measures.

Conclusion:
Green buildings and energy efficiency are essential components of addressing climate change and creating a sustainable future. By incorporating energy-efficient design, using sustainable materials, and implementing renewable energy solutions, buildings can significantly reduce their environmental footprint. Real-life examples highlight the successful implementation of green building practices, demonstrating that energy-efficient and sustainable buildings are not only achievable but also economically viable. Government policies, industry collaboration, and public awareness are vital in driving the widespread adoption of green building practices and accelerating the transition to a low carbon-built environment. Through these efforts, we can mitigate climate change, reduce energy consumption, and create healthier and more sustainable communities.

CHAPTER 12:
CIRCULAR ECONOMY AND WASTE MANAGEMENT

Introduction:
The concept of a circular economy offers a transformative approach to resource management, waste reduction, and sustainability. In this chapter, we delve into the principles of the circular economy and its role in combating climate change. We explore innovative waste management strategies, recycling initiatives, and real-life examples of circular economy practices that contribute to a more sustainable future.

1. The Circular Economy: A Paradigm Shift:
The linear economy, characterized by a take-make-dispose model, has resulted in significant resource depletion and environmental degradation. The circular economy aims to redefine this approach by emphasizing the reduction, reuse, and recycling of materials to create a closed-loop system. By keeping materials and resources in circulation for as long as possible, the circular economy minimizes waste generation and reduces the extraction of finite resources.

2. Waste Management Challenges:
Traditional waste management systems, reliant on landfilling and incineration, contribute to greenhouse gas emissions and

environmental pollution. Landfills release methane, a potent greenhouse gas, while incineration releases carbon dioxide and other harmful pollutants. The need for sustainable waste management practices has become increasingly urgent as the volume of waste continues to rise globally.

3. Reduce, Reuse, Recycle: The Three R's of the Circular Economy:
The principles of the circular economy can be encapsulated in three ways: Reduce, Reuse, and Recycle. Reducing waste at its source through conscious consumption and production practices is the first step towards a circular economy. Reusing products and materials helps extend their lifespan and minimizes the need for new resources. Recycling allows for the transformation of waste materials into new products, reducing the demand for virgin resources and mitigating environmental impacts.

4. Innovative Waste Management Strategies:
Numerous innovative waste management strategies are being implemented worldwide to promote the circular economy. These include source separation of recyclables, composting organic waste, implementing extended producer responsibility (EPR) programs, and developing advanced recycling technologies. Real-life examples such as zero waste initiatives in cities like San Francisco, California, and the implementation of bottle deposit schemes in countries like Germany and Sweden demonstrate the effectiveness of these strategies.

5. Circular Economy in Different Sectors:
The principles of the circular economy can be applied to various sectors, including manufacturing, construction, and retail. Adopting practices such as eco-design, product life extension, and remanufacturing can significantly reduce waste generation and resource consumption. Real-life examples, such as the Cradle-to-Cradle certification and the Ellen MacArthur Foundation's initiatives, highlight successful circular economy approaches in different industries.

6. Business Opportunities and Economic Benefits:
Transitioning to a circular economy offers significant business opportunities and economic benefits. By reimagining production and consumption patterns, companies can develop innovative business models, create new markets for recycled products, and enhance resource efficiency. The circular economy has the potential to generate economic growth while reducing environmental impacts.

Conclusion:
The circular economy and effective waste management are integral to addressing the challenges of climate change and resource depletion. By embracing the principles of reduce, reuse, and recycle, we can transform our linear economic model into a more sustainable and resilient system. Real-life examples demonstrate the successful implementation of circular economy practices in waste management and various sectors, paving the way for a more sustainable future. Governments, businesses, and individuals must collaborate to drive the transition to a circular economy, ensuring the efficient use of resources, waste reduction, and the mitigation of climate change impacts. Through collective action, we can create a regenerative economy that preserves the environment and fosters prosperity for present and future generations.

PART IV: CLIMATE ACTION AND POLICY

CHAPTER 13: INTERNATIONAL EFFORTS AND CLIMATE CHANGE AGREEMENTS

Introduction:
Addressing climate change requires a global effort, and international cooperation plays a crucial role in formulating effective solutions. In this chapter, we explore the international efforts and climate change agreements aimed at mitigating greenhouse gas emissions, adapting to the impacts of climate change, and fostering sustainable development. We discuss key agreements such as the Paris Agreement and examine the challenges and opportunities of global collaboration in combating climate change.

1. The Need for International Collaboration:
Climate change is a global challenge that transcends national boundaries. The interconnectedness of economies, ecosystems, and communities necessitates collective action to reduce greenhouse gas emissions and promote sustainable practices. International collaboration allows for the sharing of knowledge, resources, and best practices, facilitating the development and implementation of effective climate change strategies.

2. The Paris Agreement:

The Paris Agreement, adopted in 2015 under the United Nations Framework Convention on Climate Change (UNFCCC), is a landmark international agreement aimed at combating climate change. It sets out a framework for countries to limit global temperature rise well below 2 degrees Celsius above pre-industrial levels and pursue efforts to limit the temperature increase to 1.5 degrees Celsius. The agreement emphasizes the need for adaptation, mitigation, finance, and technology transfer to support developing countries in their climate action.

3. Nationally Determined Contributions (NDCs):

Under the Paris Agreement, countries submit their Nationally Determined Contributions (NDCs) outlining their efforts to reduce greenhouse gas emissions and adapt to climate change. NDCs vary widely in ambition and scope, reflecting each country's unique circumstances and development priorities. Real-life examples, such as Costa Rica's commitment to achieving carbon neutrality by 2050 and India's ambitious renewable energy targets, demonstrate the diverse approaches taken by countries in their NDCs.

4. Climate Finance:

Financial support plays a critical role in enabling developing countries to undertake climate change mitigation and adaptation measures. The Paris Agreement calls for developed countries to provide climate finance of at least $100 billion per year by 2020, with a commitment to further scale up this support. Initiatives such as the Green Climate Fund and the Adaptation Fund aim to mobilize funds and channel resources to support climate action in developing countries.

5. Technology Transfer and Capacity Building:

Promoting the transfer of environmentally sound technologies and building the capacity of developing countries are essential components of international climate change efforts. Technology transfer enables the adoption of clean and sustainable technologies, while capacity building enhances the skills and knowledge necessary to implement climate change initiatives effectively. Initiatives like the Technology Mechanism established under the UNFCCC support technology transfer and capacity-building activities.

6. Challenges and Opportunities:
International efforts to combat climate change face various challenges, including diverging interests, political barriers, and the complexity of negotiating global agreements. However, there are also significant opportunities for collaboration, innovation, and shared learning. The growing recognition of the economic benefits of transitioning to a low-carbon economy, the rise of renewable energy technologies, and the emergence of multilateral partnerships and initiatives demonstrate the potential for transformative change.

Conclusion:
International collaboration and climate change agreements are essential for effectively addressing the challenges of climate change. The Paris Agreement and other global efforts provide a framework for collective action, encouraging countries to take ambitious steps towards a low-carbon and resilient future. Real-life examples highlight the diverse approaches and commitments made by countries in their NDCs, showcasing the potential for transformative action. Continued international cooperation, enhanced climate finance, technology transfer, and capacity building are vital to achieving the goals outlined in these agreements and ensuring a sustainable and resilient planet for future generations. By working together, we can mitigate climate change, protect vulnerable communities, and build a more sustainable and equitable world.

CHAPTER 14: NATIONAL CLIMATE POLICIES AND LEGISLATION

Introduction:

As the impact of climate change becomes increasingly evident, countries around the world are adopting national climate policies and legislation to address this global challenge. In this chapter, we explore the importance of national-level action in battling climate change. We examine the role of governments in formulating and implementing climate policies, discuss key components of effective climate legislation, and highlight real-life examples of countries leading the way in combating climate change at the national level.

1. The Role of National Climate Policies:

National climate policies serve as a framework for countries to mitigate greenhouse gas emissions, adapt to the impacts of climate change, and transition to a low-carbon and climate-resilient economy. These policies encompass a wide range of measures, including setting emission reduction targets, promoting renewable energy and energy efficiency, implementing carbon pricing mechanisms, and fostering sustainable land and forest management.

2. Key Components of Effective Climate Legislation:

Effective climate legislation incorporates several key components that enable comprehensive and impactful action. These components may include legally binding emission reduction targets, sector-specific regulations, mechanisms for monitoring and reporting emissions, incentives for renewable energy adoption, and provisions for climate resilience and adaptation measures. By establishing clear and enforceable guidelines, the legislation provides the necessary framework to drive transformative change.

3. Real-Life Examples of National Climate Policies:
a. Germany: Germany's Energiewende (Energy Transition) policy aims to transition the country to a low-carbon economy by increasing the share of renewable energy, improving energy efficiency, and reducing greenhouse gas emissions. The policy has led to significant growth in renewable energy deployment and has positioned Germany as a global leader in renewable energy technologies.

b. Sweden: Sweden has set a target to become carbon neutral by 2045. The country has implemented various measures, including a carbon tax, investment in renewable energy sources, and promotion of electric vehicles. Sweden's efforts have resulted in a significant reduction in greenhouse gas emissions while maintaining a strong economy.

c. Costa Rica: Costa Rica has made remarkable progress in decarbonizing its economy and preserving its natural resources. The country is committed to achieving carbon neutrality by 2050 and has invested in renewable energy, reforestation, and sustainable agriculture practices. Costa Rica's achievements demonstrate the potential for small nations to lead in climate action.

4. Challenges in Implementing National Climate Policies:
Implementing national climate policies can be challenging due to various factors, including political opposition, economic to various factors, including political opposition, economic

considerations, and the need for widespread behavioural and systemic changes. Balancing short-term economic concerns with long-term sustainability goals requires careful planning and stakeholder engagement. Overcoming these challenges necessitates strong political will, collaboration between governments and stakeholders, and public awareness and support.

5. International Cooperation and Peer Learning:
International cooperation and peer learning play a crucial role in supporting the development and implementation of national climate policies. Platforms such as the United Nations Framework Convention on Climate Change (UNFCCC) provide opportunities for countries to share experiences, exchange best practices, and collaborate on climate action. Learning from successful national climate policies can inspire and inform the efforts of other countries facing similar challenges.

Conclusion:
National climate policies and legislation are essential for driving meaningful action in the fight against climate change. Real-life examples demonstrate the diverse approaches taken by countries, showcasing the potential for transformative change in reducing greenhouse gas emissions, promoting renewable energy, and enhancing resilience. Despite challenges, national-level action holds immense promise for creating a sustainable and climate-resilient future. By adopting and implementing effective climate policies, countries can lead the way in combating climate change, protecting vulnerable communities, and ensuring a sustainable planet for future generations.

CHAPTER 15: LOCAL GOVERNMENTS AND COMMUNITY INITIATIVES

Introduction:
In the face of the climate crisis, local governments and community initiatives play a crucial role in driving climate action and resilience at the grassroots level. This chapter explores the significant impact that local governments and communities can have in battling climate change. We delve into the innovative solutions and collaborative efforts undertaken by local governments, as well as the inspiring initiatives led by communities worldwide to mitigate greenhouse gas emissions, adapt to climate impacts, and build climate-resilient societies.

1. The Power of Local Action:
Local governments are uniquely positioned to address climate change as they have direct influence over land use, transportation, infrastructure, and waste management within their jurisdictions. They can implement climate policies and regulations tailored to their specific contexts, encouraging sustainable practices, and fostering community engagement. Local action can catalyse broader change and inspire other regions to follow suit.

2. Community-Led Initiatives:
Communities have the potential to drive meaningful change by

actively participating in climate action. Grassroots initiatives, led by passionate individuals or organizations, can promote sustainable practices, raise awareness, and empower community members to take ownership of climate solutions. These initiatives range from community gardens and renewable energy cooperatives to waste reduction programs and eco-friendly transportation projects.

3. Real-Life Examples of Local Governments and Community Initiatives:

a. City of Copenhagen, Denmark: Copenhagen has set ambitious goals to become carbon-neutral by 2025. The city has implemented an extensive cycling infrastructure, invested in renewable energy, and transformed urban spaces to prioritize pedestrians and cyclists. These efforts have significantly reduced the city's carbon footprint while creating a liveable and sustainable urban environment.

b. Transition Town Movement, Totnes, UK: The Transition Town movement began in Totnes, UK, and has since spread to numerous communities worldwide. It focuses on building resilient, low-carbon communities by promoting local food production, renewable energy, and sustainable transportation. Transition Town initiatives empower communities to come together and envision a sustainable future.

c. The Blue Community Project, Victoria, Canada: The Blue Community Project encourages communities to prioritize water sustainability by phasing out bottled water, promoting public access to water, and implementing water conservation measures. The initiative has gained traction globally, with various communities adopting its principles to protect water resources and reduce plastic waste.

4. Collaborative Networks and Support:
Local governments and community initiatives often benefit from collaboration and support networks. Regional and global

organizations provide resources, knowledge-sharing platforms, and funding opportunities to assist in climate action at the local level. Collaborative networks enable cities and communities to learn from each other, share best practices, and amplify their impact.

5. Policy Advocacy and Grassroots Movements:
Local governments and community initiatives can also advocate for policy changes at higher levels of government. Grassroots movements, such as youth-led climate strikes and citizen lobbying groups, raise awareness and apply pressure on policymakers to take more ambitious action on climate change. These efforts are essential in shaping political will and driving systemic change.

Conclusion:
Local governments and community initiatives play a vital role in addressing the climate crisis. Through their actions, they demonstrate the potential for transformative change at the grassroots level. Real-life examples of cities and communities leading the way inspire others to act and contribute to the global fight against climate change. By harnessing the power of local action, communities can build climate-resilient societies, reduce greenhouse gas emissions, and create a sustainable future for generations to come. It is through the collective efforts of individuals, communities, and local governments that we can tackle the climate crisis and build a more sustainable and equitable world.

CHAPTER 16: CORPORATE RESPONSIBILITY AND SUSTAINABLE BUSINESS PRACTICES

Introduction:

In the fight against climate change, the role of corporations is pivotal. This chapter explores how businesses can contribute to battling climate change through corporate responsibility and sustainable practices. We delve into the importance of corporate sustainability, discuss the benefits of integrating climate-conscious strategies into business operations, and highlight real-life examples of companies leading the way in sustainable practices.

1. The Business Case for Sustainability:

Embracing sustainability is not only crucial for the planet but also makes good business sense. Companies that prioritize sustainable practices can gain a competitive edge, enhance brand reputation, attract environmentally conscious consumers, and improve operational efficiency. By considering the long-term impacts of their operations, companies can create value for shareholders while minimizing their environmental footprint.

2. Sustainable Supply Chains:

One area where companies can have a significant impact on climate change is through sustainable supply chain management. By collaborating with suppliers, businesses can implement environmentally responsible practices such as reducing carbon emissions, minimizing waste, and ensuring ethical sourcing. Sustainable supply chains not only reduce environmental impact but also enhance resilience and reduce risks in the face of climate-related disruptions.

3. Renewable Energy and Energy Efficiency:
Many companies are embracing renewable energy sources and implementing energy-efficient measures to reduce their carbon footprint. Transitioning to renewable energy not only reduces greenhouse gas emissions but also provides long-term cost savings and energy security. Investments in energy-efficient technologies and practices can lead to significant reductions in energy consumption and operational expenses.

4. Carbon Offsetting and Net Zero Goals:
Companies can take responsibility for their carbon emissions by implementing carbon offsetting programs and setting ambitious net-zero goals. Carbon offsetting involves investing in projects that reduce or remove greenhouse gas emissions, such as reforestation or renewable energy projects, to offset their emissions. By committing to net-zero emissions, companies demonstrate their dedication to combating climate change and contributing to a low-carbon future.

5. Collaboration and Partnerships:
Corporate responsibility extends beyond individual companies. Collaborative efforts and partnerships between businesses, NGOs, and governments can amplify the impact of sustainable practices. Initiatives such as industry-wide sustainability certifications, collaborative research projects, and joint advocacy efforts can drive systemic change and accelerate the transition to a sustainable economy.

6. Real-Life Examples:

a. Unilever: Unilever is committed to achieving net-zero emissions from its products by 2039. The company has implemented sustainable sourcing practices, reduced its greenhouse gas emissions, and invested in renewable energy. Unilever's Sustainable Living Plan demonstrates how a large multinational corporation can prioritize sustainability while driving business growth.

b. Patagonia: Patagonia is known for its commitment to environmental sustainability. The company promotes fair trade, uses recycled materials in its products, and invests in renewable energy. Patagonia's transparent supply chain and advocacy for environmental causes have positioned it as a leader in sustainable business practices.

c. Interface: Interface, a global modular flooring company, has set ambitious sustainability goals, including a mission to have zero negative impact on the environment by 2020. The company has made significant progress in reducing its carbon footprint, water usage, and waste generation through innovative manufacturing processes and product design.

Conclusion:

Corporate responsibility and sustainable business practices are essential for combatting climate change. By integrating sustainability into their operations, businesses can contribute to a low-carbon economy while reaping benefits such as cost savings, enhanced brand reputation, and resilience to climate-related risks. Real-life examples demonstrate the transformative power of corporate sustainability and inspire other businesses to adopt climate-conscious strategies. As corporations continue to prioritize sustainability, they play a crucial role in driving the global transition to a more sustainable and resilient future.

PART V: ADAPTING TO A CHANGING CLIMATE

CHAPTER 17:
CLIMATE RESILIENCE AND ADAPTATION STRATEGIES

Introduction:

As the impacts of climate change intensify, it is essential to develop resilience and adaptation strategies to protect communities, ecosystems, and economies. This chapter explores the importance of climate resilience and discusses various strategies that can help societies and ecosystems adapt to the changing climate. Real-life examples demonstrate the effectiveness of these strategies and inspire proactive action.

1. Understanding Climate Resilience:

Climate resilience refers to the ability of individuals, communities, and systems to anticipate, withstand, recover, and adapt to the impacts of climate change. It involves building adaptive capacity, reducing vulnerability, and ensuring the long-term sustainability of social, economic, and ecological systems.

2. Enhancing Natural Resilience:

Protecting and restoring natural ecosystems can enhance their resilience to climate change. For instance, conserving forests, wetlands, and coral reefs can help mitigate the impacts of storms, floods, and sea-level rise. Ecosystem-based adaptation strategies, such as restoring mangrove forests to act as natural buffers against coastal erosion and storm surges, have proven effective in increasing resilience in vulnerable regions.

3. Climate-Resilient Infrastructure:
Designing and implementing climate-resilient infrastructure is crucial for minimizing the vulnerability of communities to climate-related hazards. This includes constructing buildings that can withstand extreme weather events, developing robust stormwater management systems, and adapting transportation networks to changing climate patterns. Examples of climate-resilient infrastructure can be found in cities that incorporate green roofs, permeable pavements, and flood-resistant infrastructure.

4. Agriculture and Food Security:
Farmers and agricultural workers are at the forefront of climate change impacts. Climate-resilient agricultural practices, such as conservation agriculture, agroforestry, and precision farming, can help increase agricultural productivity while reducing vulnerability to extreme weather events. Diversifying crops, improving water management, and using climate-resilient seeds are examples of adaptation strategies that can enhance food security.

5. Community-Based Adaptation:
Engaging local communities in climate resilience efforts is crucial for effective adaptation. Community-based adaptation initiatives involve empowering local communities to identify climate risks, develop adaptation strategies, and implement projects that address their specific vulnerabilities. Examples include community-led reforestation projects, the establishment of early warning systems for natural disasters, and the creation of local climate action plans.

6. Resilience in Urban Areas:
Urban areas are particularly vulnerable to climate change impacts. Implementing climate-resilient urban planning and

design can enhance the capacity of cities to withstand and recover from climate-related events. This may involve incorporating green spaces, promoting sustainable transportation options, and implementing climate-responsive building codes.

7. Financing Resilience:
Funding climate resilience initiatives is critical for their successful implementation. Governments, international organizations, and financial institutions play a vital role in providing financial resources to support adaptation projects. For instance, the Green Climate Fund supports climate-resilient initiatives in developing countries, helping them build resilience and adapt to changing climate conditions.

Conclusion:
Climate resilience and adaptation strategies are essential for communities, ecosystems, and economies to effectively respond to the impacts of climate change. By implementing nature-based solutions, climate-resilient infrastructure, and community-led initiatives, societies can build resilience and reduce vulnerability. Real-life examples demonstrate the successful implementation of these strategies and inspire further action to address the challenges posed by climate change. Investing in climate resilience today is crucial for ensuring a sustainable and secure future for generations to come.

CHAPTER 18: WATER CONSERVATION AND MANAGEMENT

Introduction:
Water is a vital resource for agriculture, ecosystems, and human well-being, but it is also highly vulnerable to the impacts of climate change. This chapter explores the importance of water conservation and management in the context of climate change. It discusses the challenges faced by farmers and agricultural workers, as well as the strategies and technologies they employ to ensure efficient water use and sustainable practices. Real-life examples demonstrate the effectiveness of these approaches and inspire collective action towards water conservation and management.

1. Understanding the Water Challenge:
Climate change exacerbates water scarcity, with changing rainfall patterns and increased evaporation rates. Farmers and agricultural workers face the challenge of managing water resources to sustain crop production while minimizing water wastage. The availability and quality of water directly impact food security, livelihoods, and ecosystem health.

2. Efficient Irrigation Techniques:
Adopting efficient irrigation techniques is crucial for reducing water consumption in agriculture. Drip irrigation, precision sprinklers, and micro-sprinklers deliver water directly to plant

roots, minimizing evaporation and runoff. These methods can significantly improve water-use efficiency and crop yields, as demonstrated by farmers using drip irrigation systems in arid regions such as Israel and Australia.

3. Crop Selection and Water Demand:
Choosing appropriate crop varieties that are well-adapted to local conditions and require less water can contribute to water conservation. Farmers can select drought-tolerant crops and employ agronomic practices such as intercropping and crop rotation to maximize water efficiency. For example, in water-stressed regions of India, farmers have shifted from water-intensive rice cultivation to less water-demanding crops like millet.

4. Water Harvesting and Storage:
Rainwater harvesting and storage systems capture and store rainfall for agricultural use during dry periods. Techniques such as building small-scale reservoirs, ponds, and rainwater harvesting structures enable farmers to collect and utilize water effectively. In regions like Rajasthan, India, where water scarcity is a major concern, community-led water harvesting projects have successfully restored groundwater levels and supported agricultural activities.

5. Integrated Water Management:
Integrated water management approaches consider the entire water cycle, including rainwater, surface water, and groundwater, to ensure efficient and sustainable water use. This involves implementing watershed management practices, promoting water-efficient technologies, and establishing water rights and governance systems. The Murray-Darling Basin in Australia is an example of integrated water management, where multiple stakeholders collaborate to balance water allocations and protect the ecological health of the basin.

6. Climate-Resilient Agriculture:

Climate-resilient agricultural practices promote sustainable water management by enhancing soil health and moisture retention capacity. Conservation agriculture, agroforestry, and mulching techniques help improve soil structure, reduce evaporation, and increase water infiltration. These practices contribute to long-term water conservation and support agricultural productivity even in the face of climate variability.

7. Community Engagement and Water Conservation:
Community participation and awareness are essential for successful water conservation efforts. Farmers, local communities, and water management authorities can collaborate to develop water management plans, share best practices, and promote water-saving behaviours. Community-driven initiatives like water user associations in Nepal and participatory watershed management programs in Ethiopia have demonstrated the power of collective action in water conservation.

Conclusion:
Water conservation and management are critical components of climate change adaptation in agriculture. Through efficient irrigation techniques, crop selection, water harvesting, integrated water management, and community engagement, farmers and agricultural workers can play a vital role in reducing water consumption and ensuring sustainable water use. Real-life examples demonstrate the positive outcomes of these strategies, such as increased water-use efficiency, improved crop yields, and enhanced resilience to climate change. By prioritizing water conservation and management, we can protect this valuable resource, support agricultural livelihoods, and build a more sustainable future in the face of the climate crisis.

CHAPTER 19: PROTECTING BIODIVERSITY AND ECOSYSTEMS

Introduction:

Biodiversity and healthy ecosystems play a crucial role in mitigating and adapting to climate change. In this chapter, we explore the impact of climate change on biodiversity and ecosystems and discuss the efforts of farmers and agricultural workers in protecting and restoring these vital natural systems. Real-life examples demonstrate the importance of safeguarding biodiversity and ecosystems and inspire actions to preserve and enhance their resilience in the face of climate change.

1. Climate Change and Biodiversity Loss:

Climate change poses significant threats to biodiversity, leading to species loss, habitat degradation, and disruption of ecological processes. Changes in temperature and precipitation patterns can impact the distribution and behaviour of species, affecting ecosystem dynamics. For instance, the bleaching of coral reefs due to rising sea temperatures has devastating consequences for marine biodiversity.

2. Conserving and Restoring Natural Habitats:

Farmers and agricultural workers can contribute to biodiversity conservation by protecting and restoring natural habitats within and around agricultural landscapes. This can involve preserving native vegetation, creating wildlife corridors, and implementing agroecological practices that promote biodiversity. The adoption of organic farming methods and the establishment of buffer zones are examples of on-farm practices that enhance habitat connectivity and support diverse plant and animal species.

3. Sustainable Land Management:
Implementing sustainable land management practices is essential for protecting biodiversity and ecosystems. This includes techniques such as agroforestry, which integrates trees with crops and livestock, providing habitat for wildlife, preventing soil erosion, and enhancing biodiversity. Agroecological approaches, such as integrated pest management and crop rotation, minimize the use of agrochemicals, reduce soil degradation, and promote beneficial insects and microorganisms.

4. Ecosystem-based Adaptation:
Ecosystem-based adaptation (EbA) strategies utilize the inherent resilience of ecosystems to build climate resilience. Farmers and agricultural workers can implement EbA approaches by restoring wetlands, creating green infrastructure, and protecting natural water sources. For example, the conservation and restoration of mangrove forests in coastal areas help mitigate the impacts of climate change, reduce coastal erosion, and provide habitats for marine species.

5. Sustainable Fisheries and Aquaculture:
Climate change affects marine ecosystems and fisheries, disrupting fish migration patterns and altering oceanic conditions. Sustainable fisheries and responsible aquaculture practices are vital for protecting marine biodiversity. Implementation of ecosystem-based fisheries management, the establishment of marine protected areas, and the promotion of sustainable aquaculture techniques, such as integrated multi-trophic aquaculture, contribute to the conservation of marine biodiversity.

6. Community-led Conservation Initiatives:
Community-led conservation initiatives play a crucial role in protecting biodiversity and ecosystems. Local communities, farmers, and indigenous groups have a deep understanding of their ecosystems and can contribute to sustainable resource management. Collaborative efforts, such as community-managed forests in Nepal and indigenous-led conservation projects in the Amazon rainforest, demonstrate the effectiveness of community-based conservation in preserving biodiversity and cultural heritage.

Conclusion:
Protecting biodiversity and ecosystems is essential for building resilience to climate change and ensuring the long-term sustainability of agriculture and food systems. Farmers and agricultural workers play a vital role in safeguarding and restoring biodiversity through sustainable land management practices, habitat conservation, and community-led initiatives. Real-life examples illustrate the positive outcomes of these efforts, including enhanced ecosystem services, increased biodiversity, and improved climate resilience. By prioritizing the protection of biodiversity and ecosystems, we can secure a more sustainable future for both human well-being and the planet.

CHAPTER 20: FOOD SECURITY AND SUSTAINABLE AGRICULTURE

Introduction:

In this chapter, we explore the critical role of farmers and agricultural workers in battling climate change and ensuring food security through sustainable agricultural practices. We delve into the challenges posed by climate change to global food production and discuss innovative solutions and real-life examples of sustainable agriculture that promote resilience, productivity, and food security in the face of a changing climate.

1. Climate Change and Food Security:

Climate change poses significant threats to global food security. Rising temperatures, changing rainfall patterns, and extreme weather events can lead to reduced crop yields, increased pests and diseases, and disruptions in food production and distribution. Smallholder farmers, who are often more vulnerable to climate change impacts, play a crucial role in ensuring food security for their communities and beyond.

2. Climate-Smart Agriculture:

Climate-smart agriculture (CSA) focuses on enhancing agricultural productivity, building resilience, and reducing greenhouse gas emissions. CSA practices include sustainable land management, water conservation, agroforestry, and precision farming techniques. For instance, conservation agriculture, which involves minimal soil disturbance, permanent soil cover, and crop rotation, helps retain soil moisture, reduce erosion, and increase crop productivity.

3. Diversification and Crop Resilience:
Farmers can enhance their resilience to climate change by diversifying their crop portfolios. By cultivating a range of crops that have different tolerance levels to heat, drought, or flooding, farmers reduce the risk of complete crop failure. For example, in regions prone to drought, farmers may adopt drought-tolerant crop varieties such as millet or sorghum alongside traditional staple crops.

4. Agroecology and Regenerative Agriculture:
Agroecology and regenerative agriculture emphasize ecological principles and the integration of natural processes into farming systems. These approaches promote soil health, biodiversity conservation, and sustainable resource management. Techniques such as organic farming, crop rotation, cover cropping, and the use of compost and manure contribute to soil fertility, reduce chemical inputs, and enhance ecosystem services.

5. Conservation Agriculture and No-Till Farming:
Conservation agriculture and no-till farming practices minimize soil disturbance and promote soil health and carbon sequestration. By leaving crop residues on the field and reducing tillage, farmers can improve water retention, enhance soil structure, and reduce greenhouse gas emissions. This approach has been successfully adopted by farmers around the world, such as those in Brazil's Cerrado region.

6. Farmer-Led Adaptation and Knowledge Sharing:
Farmers and agricultural workers are at the forefront of adaptation to climate change. Through farmer-led initiatives and knowledge-sharing networks, they exchange practices and

strategies to cope with climate variability. For example, farmer field schools in sub-Saharan Africa have empowered farmers to experiment with climate-resilient practices and share their experiences with their communities.

Conclusion:
Farmers and agricultural workers are vital agents in battling climate change and ensuring global food security. Sustainable agriculture practices such as climate-smart agriculture, agroecology, and regenerative farming, enhance resilience, promote biodiversity, and reduce greenhouse gas emissions. Real-life examples from around the world demonstrate the success of these approaches in improving productivity, conserving natural resources, and securing food for present and future generations. By investing in sustainable agriculture and supporting farmers' efforts, we can build a more food-secure and resilient future in the face of climate change.

PART VI: THE HUMAN ELEMENT

CHAPTER 21: CLIMATE JUSTICE AND EQUITY

Introduction:
In this chapter, we delve into the critical issue of climate justice and equity in the context of farmers and agricultural workers battling climate change. We explore the disproportionate impacts of climate change on vulnerable communities and discuss the importance of addressing social, economic, and environmental inequalities in climate action. Real-life examples highlight initiatives that strive for climate justice and equitable solutions in the agricultural sector.

1. Inequitable Climate Impacts:
Climate change disproportionately affects marginalized communities, including smallholder farmers, indigenous peoples, and rural populations. These groups often have limited resources, access to information, and political power to mitigate and adapt to climate change. As a result, they are more vulnerable to food insecurity, displacement, and loss of livelihoods.

2. Climate-Induced Migration and Displacement:
Rising sea levels, droughts, and extreme weather events force many farmers and agricultural workers to migrate from rural areas to urban centres or other regions. This migration, driven by climate-related factors, puts additional strain on urban infrastructure, increases competition for resources, and exacerbates social and economic disparities. Efforts to address climate-induced migration must prioritize the needs and rights of affected communities.

3. Community-Based Adaptation:
Community-based adaptation approaches recognize the knowledge and resilience of local communities in responding to climate change. These initiatives empower communities to develop and implement their strategies, based on their unique socio-cultural and ecological contexts. For example, in Bangladesh, the "Char Development and Settlement Project" supports climate-resilient agricultural practices and infrastructure development in riverine islands.

4. Gender and Climate Justice:
Gender plays a significant role in climate justice. Women, particularly in developing countries, are often disproportionately affected by climate change due to their roles in agriculture and household management. Empowering women through access to resources, education, and decision-making processes not only promotes gender equality but also strengthens resilience and adaptation capacities at the community level.

5. Climate Finance and Support for Vulnerable Communities:
International climate finance mechanisms aim to support adaptation and mitigation efforts in developing countries. However, there is a need for a more equitable distribution of funds and resources to ensure that vulnerable communities receive adequate support. Initiatives like the Green Climate Fund and the Adaptation Fund are working towards channelling funds to projects that prioritize climate justice and community empowerment.

6. Indigenous Knowledge and Traditional Practices:
Indigenous communities possess valuable knowledge and traditional practices that contribute to climate resilience. Their traditional ecological knowledge, sustainable land management techniques, and diverse agricultural practices can offer insights into climate adaptation and mitigation strategies. Collaborative partnerships between indigenous communities and scientists

can foster knowledge exchange and ensure that indigenous perspectives are integrated into climate policies.

Conclusion:
Climate justice and equity are essential considerations in the fight against climate change, particularly in the agricultural sector. By acknowledging and addressing the unequal impacts of climate change on vulnerable communities, we can work towards inclusive and equitable solutions. Real-life examples demonstrate the importance of community-based adaptation, gender empowerment, climate finance, and the incorporation of indigenous knowledge. By prioritizing climate justice and equity, we can create a more just and sustainable future for farmers, agricultural workers, and all those affected by the climate crisis.

CHAPTER 22: HEALTH IMPACTS OF CLIMATE CHANGE

Introduction:

In this chapter, we explore the significant health impacts of climate change and the challenges faced by farmers and agricultural workers as they battle these consequences. We examine the direct and indirect health effects of climate change, including heat-related illnesses, vector-borne diseases, malnutrition, and mental health issues. Real-life examples illustrate the severity of these impacts and highlight initiatives that prioritize the health and well-being of farmers and agricultural communities.

1. Heat-Related Illnesses:

Rising temperatures due to climate change pose a significant threat to the health of farmers and agricultural workers. Prolonged exposure to extreme heat can lead to heat exhaustion, heatstroke, and other heat-related illnesses. In regions with hot climates, such as South Asia, farm labourers face increased risks, especially during peak agricultural seasons. Heat stress reduction strategies, such as providing shaded rest areas and implementing work-hour restrictions, can help protect workers from these hazards.

2. Vector-Borne Diseases:

Climate change influences the distribution and behaviour of

disease-carrying vectors, such as mosquitoes and ticks, leading to an increased incidence of vector-borne diseases. Malaria, dengue fever, and Lyme disease are examples of illnesses that can impact agricultural communities. For instance, in Sub-Saharan Africa, changing rainfall patterns contribute to the spread of malaria. Integrated vector management approaches, including vector surveillance and control measures, are crucial for reducing the burden of vector-borne diseases.

3. Food Security and Malnutrition:
Climate change disrupts agricultural productivity and food systems, leading to food shortages and malnutrition. Farmers face challenges such as unpredictable rainfall patterns, droughts, and floods, which affect crop yields and livestock productivity. In turn, food insecurity and malnutrition can contribute to various health issues, particularly among vulnerable populations. Sustainable agricultural practices, climate-resilient crop varieties, and social safety nets can help ensure food security and improve nutritional outcomes.

4. Mental Health and Well-being:
The impacts of climate change, such as extreme weather events and agricultural losses, can cause significant psychological distress and impact mental health. Farmers and agricultural workers often experience anxiety, depression, and stress as they navigate the uncertainties and challenges posed by climate change. Community support systems, access to mental health services, and resilience-building programs can help address these mental health concerns and enhance overall well-being.

5. Climate Change Adaptation and Health Resilience:
Efforts to build resilience in agricultural communities should include strategies that prioritize health considerations. This involves implementing early warning systems for extreme weather events, improving access to clean water and sanitation, promoting disease prevention measures, and strengthening health infrastructure in rural areas. Additionally, integrating

climate change and health considerations into national policies and plans is essential for effective adaptation and mitigation strategies.

Conclusion:
The health impacts of climate change pose significant challenges for farmers and agricultural workers. Addressing these impacts requires a multi-sectoral approach that integrates climate change adaptation, health resilience, and sustainable agricultural practices. Real-life examples demonstrate the importance of heat stress reduction, vector-borne disease management, food security measures, mental health support, and climate-smart health policies. By prioritizing the health and well-being of farmers and agricultural communities, we can mitigate the adverse health effects of climate change and build a more resilient future.

CHAPTER 23: MIGRATION AND CLIMATE REFUGEES

Introduction:
In this chapter, we delve into the complex issue of migration and the displacement of people due to climate change. We explore how climate change contributes to forced migration, the challenges faced by climate refugees, and the importance of addressing this humanitarian crisis. Real-life examples highlight the experiences of communities affected by climate-related displacement and the urgent need for sustainable solutions.

1. Climate-Induced Displacement:
Climate change exacerbates existing environmental, social, and economic vulnerabilities, leading to the displacement of people from their homes and communities. Rising sea levels, droughts, floods, and extreme weather events are among the factors that force individuals and communities to seek safer and more sustainable living conditions. The Pacific Islands, for example, are grappling with the prospect of entire nations becoming uninhabitable due to sea-level rise.

2. Challenges Faced by Climate Refugees:
Climate refugees often face multiple challenges, including loss of livelihoods, social disruption, inadequate access to resources, and limited legal protections. They may encounter difficulties in finding new homes, integrating into new communities,

and accessing basic services such as healthcare and education. Climate-related displacement can also lead to social tensions and conflicts, further exacerbating the hardships faced by affected populations.

3. International Legal Frameworks:
The legal status and protection of climate refugees remain complex and insufficiently addressed within existing international frameworks. The 1951 Refugee Convention primarily focuses on persecution-based displacement rather than environmental factors. However, the United Nations Framework Convention on Climate Change (UNFCCC) recognizes the importance of addressing climate-related migration and advocates for cooperation and assistance to affected communities.

4. Resilient Communities and Sustainable Solutions:
Building resilient communities in the face of climate change is crucial for mitigating displacement and supporting affected populations. This involves implementing adaptation strategies, promoting sustainable land and water management practices, and investing in climate-resilient infrastructure. Supporting sustainable agriculture and livelihood diversification can also enhance the resilience of rural communities and reduce the need for migration.

5. International Cooperation and Assistance:
Addressing the challenges of climate-induced migration requires international cooperation and assistance. Developed nations have a responsibility to provide financial and technological support to vulnerable countries and communities. The Global Compact on Migration and the Platform on Disaster Displacement are initiatives that aim to facilitate international cooperation and coordination on climate-related migration issues.

Real-Life Examples:
Real-life examples of climate-related displacement include the

inhabitants of the Carteret Islands in Papua New Guinea, who are being relocated due to rising sea levels. In Bangladesh, communities are being forced to migrate as the country faces increased flooding and cyclones. The Kiribati government has purchased land in Fiji as a potential future home for its displaced population. These examples illustrate the urgent need for comprehensive solutions to protect the rights and well-being of climate refugees.

Conclusion:
Climate-induced migration poses significant challenges for affected individuals, communities, and nations. It requires a coordinated and compassionate response from the international community, with a focus on addressing the root causes of climate change, supporting adaptation and resilience efforts, and providing legal protections and assistance to climate refugees. By recognizing the human rights of climate-displaced populations and implementing sustainable solutions, we can alleviate the suffering of those forced to leave their homes and build a more just and resilient future for all.

CHAPTER 24: YOUTH ACTIVISM AND THE FIGHT FOR A SUSTAINABLE FUTURE

Introduction:

In this chapter, we explore the inspiring role of youth activism in addressing the challenges of climate change and building a sustainable future. We delve into the reasons behind the rise of youth climate movements, highlight the impactful actions taken by young activists, and discuss the importance of empowering youth in shaping climate policies and promoting sustainable practices.

1. The Rise of Youth Climate Movements:

Over the past decade, young people around the world have mobilized and taken to the streets to demand urgent action on climate change. The youth-led movements, such as Fridays for Future, Sunrise Movement, and Extinction Rebellion, have garnered significant attention and galvanized public support for climate action. These movements highlight the moral imperative of addressing climate change and demand accountability from governments and corporations.

2. Youth Activists Taking Action:

Youth activists have not only raised awareness about climate change but have also initiated concrete actions to combat its impacts. They have organized strikes, protests, and demonstrations, pushing for policies that prioritize renewable energy, sustainable agriculture, and carbon neutrality. Young activists have also been at the forefront of initiatives like tree-planting campaigns, plastic waste reduction, and community-led sustainable projects.

3. Real-Life Examples of Youth Climate Activism:
Greta Thunberg, a Swedish teenager, gained international recognition for her solo school strike for climate action. Her activism has inspired millions of young people worldwide to join the fight against climate change. Other examples include Isra Hirsi, co-founder of the U.S.-based youth-led organization US Youth Climate Strike, and Vanessa Nakate, a Ugandan climate activist who advocates for climate justice and amplifies the voices of African youth.

4. Empowering Youth in Climate Decision-Making:
Youth involvement in climate decision-making processes is crucial for shaping effective policies and promoting sustainable practices. Governments, organizations, and institutions should create platforms for meaningful youth participation, such as youth advisory boards, mentorship programs, and funding opportunities for youth-led initiatives. By including young voices, decision-makers can tap into innovative ideas and ensure intergenerational equity.

5. Educational and Awareness-Building Initiatives:
Education plays a pivotal role in empowering youth to become climate activists and change agents. Integrating climate change education into school curricula and providing access to information and resources equips young people with the knowledge and skills to understand and address the climate crisis. Youth-led awareness campaigns, workshops, and conferences also facilitate knowledge sharing and encourage collective action.

Real-Life Examples:

The School Strike for Climate movement, initiated by Greta Thunberg, has seen students worldwide staging strikes and demanding climate action from their governments. The Sunrise Movement in the United States has successfully pushed for the Green New Deal, an ambitious policy framework to address climate change and economic inequality. These examples highlight the power of youth activism in influencing policy agendas and driving societal change.

Conclusion:

Youth activism has emerged as a powerful force in the fight against climate change, driving momentum for sustainable solutions and demanding accountability from leaders. Young people are demonstrating their determination, resilience, and innovation in tackling the climate crisis. By empowering youth, fostering their engagement in decision-making, and amplifying their voices, we can create a more sustainable future that prioritizes the well-being of both present and future generations. Together, let us celebrate and support the youth activists who are leading the way toward a more sustainable and just world.

PART VII: INSPIRING CHANGE

CHAPTER 25: SUCCESS STORIES AND POSITIVE IMPACTS

Introduction:

In this chapter, we highlight success stories and the positive impacts of farmers and agricultural workers who have taken proactive steps to battle climate change. Through innovative practices and sustainable approaches, they are not only mitigating the effects of climate change but also making significant contributions to environmental conservation, community resilience, and food security.

1. Sustainable Agriculture Practices:

Farmers and agricultural workers are implementing sustainable farming practices that promote soil health, water conservation, and biodiversity. Examples include agroforestry, which combines trees with crops to improve soil fertility and increase carbon sequestration, and precision agriculture techniques that optimize resource use and reduce greenhouse gas emissions. These practices not only reduce the carbon footprint of agriculture but also enhance the resilience of farming systems.

2. Climate-Smart Crop Cultivation:

Farmers are adapting their crop choices and cultivation techniques to changing climatic conditions. They are incorporating drought-resistant varieties, adopting precision irrigation systems, and implementing crop rotation strategies to enhance soil fertility. These climate-smart approaches increase crop resilience, reduce water consumption, and improve yields, ensuring food security in the face of climate change.

3. Organic and Regenerative Farming:
Farmers are transitioning to organic and regenerative farming practices, minimizing the use of synthetic inputs and prioritizing soil health. Organic farming reduces the reliance on chemical pesticides and fertilizers, while regenerative farming focuses on restoring soil health through practices like cover cropping and crop rotation. These approaches sequester carbon, enhance biodiversity, and improve the overall sustainability of agricultural systems.

4. Community-Led Adaptation:
Farmers and agricultural workers are actively engaging in community-led adaptation initiatives. They participate in knowledge-sharing networks, farmer field schools, and collaborative projects to exchange information and implement climate-smart practices. By working together, they build resilient communities, share resources, and collectively address the challenges posed by climate change.

5. Value-Chain Innovations:
Farmers and agricultural workers are exploring innovative value-chain approaches to reduce post-harvest losses, increase market access, and improve profitability. These include establishing farmer cooperatives, implementing sustainable packaging and transportation systems, and promoting fair trade practices. These initiatives not only benefit farmers economically but also contribute to reducing food waste and carbon emissions along the supply chain.

Real-Life Examples:
The SRI (System of Rice Intensification) technique, adopted by rice farmers in various countries, has significantly reduced water usage and increased yields. In India, the Zero Budget

Natural Farming model has empowered farmers to adopt organic practices, leading to improved soil health and reduced production costs. The Farmer Managed Natural Regeneration project in Niger has restored degraded land and increased agricultural productivity, benefiting both farmers and the environment.

Conclusion:
Farmers and agricultural workers are at the forefront of climate change adaptation and mitigation efforts. Their sustainable farming practices, resilience-building initiatives, and innovations along the value chain are creating positive impacts on the environment, communities, and food security. By sharing success stories and supporting these efforts, we can inspire others to adopt similar practices and accelerate the transition to a more sustainable and climate-resilient agricultural sector. The collective actions of farmers and agricultural workers demonstrate the power of local solutions and highlight the crucial role they play in combating climate change and securing a sustainable future for generations to come.

CHAPTER 26: INNOVATIVE SOLUTIONS FROM GRASSROOTS MOVEMENTS

Introduction:
In this chapter, we explore the inspiring efforts of grassroots movements and organizations in the agricultural sector that are actively working to combat climate change. These initiatives are driven by local communities, farmers, and agricultural workers who are implementing innovative solutions to address the challenges posed by a changing climate. Their creative approaches, often rooted in traditional knowledge and sustainable practices, are making a significant impact on both the environment and local communities.

1. Farmer-to-Farmer Knowledge Exchange:
Grassroots movements facilitate knowledge exchange among farmers, enabling them to learn from one another's experiences and adopt sustainable farming practices. These platforms connect farmers who have successfully implemented climate-resilient techniques, such as agroecology or permaculture, with those seeking guidance. This farmer-to-farmer knowledge exchange helps spread best practices and empowers farmers to make

informed decisions.

2. Seed Conservation and Diversity:
Grassroots movements are actively involved in seed conservation and promoting the use of traditional and locally adapted crop varieties. They work with farmers to preserve indigenous seeds that have adapted to local climatic conditions and are more resilient to climate change impacts. By maintaining seed diversity, these initiatives contribute to food security, biodiversity conservation, and the resilience of agricultural systems.

3. Community Seed Banks:
Community seed banks are established by grassroots organizations to safeguard local seed varieties and ensure their availability to farmers. These seed banks provide farmers with access to diverse and climate-resilient seeds, enabling them to adapt to changing environmental conditions. They also play a crucial role in preserving traditional knowledge associated with seed selection and cultivation.

4. Climate-Resilient Farming Techniques:
Grassroots movements promote and disseminate climate-resilient farming techniques that help farmers adapt to climate change. These techniques include rainwater harvesting, conservation agriculture, and integrated pest management. By implementing these practices, farmers can enhance water use efficiency, improve soil health, and reduce dependence on chemical inputs.

5. Farmer-led Research and Innovation:
Farmers and agricultural workers involved in grassroots movements are often engaged in participatory research and innovation. They collaborate with scientists, researchers, and extension services to develop context-specific solutions to climate-related challenges. Through on-farm experiments and trials, they test and refine climate-smart practices, demonstrating the potential for sustainable agriculture.

Real-Life Examples:
The Deccan Development Society in India supports women farmers in practising sustainable agriculture and preserving traditional seeds, promoting food sovereignty and climate resilience. The Slow Food movement works globally to protect local food cultures and biodiversity, encouraging sustainable farming practices. The Farmer Field School approach, implemented by various organizations worldwide, empowers farmers to experiment with climate-smart practices and collectively learn from their experiences.

Conclusion:
Grassroots movements and organizations are driving change at the local level by fostering innovation, knowledge exchange, and community engagement. Their initiatives promote sustainable agriculture, preserve traditional knowledge, and build climate resilience among farmers and agricultural workers. By highlighting these innovative solutions, we can inspire and encourage broader adoption of grassroots approaches to combat climate change. These movements serve as powerful examples of how local action and community empowerment can contribute to global efforts in mitigating climate change and creating a more sustainable future for agriculture and the planet as a whole.

CHAPTER 27: EMPOWERING INDIVIDUALS TO TAKE ACTION

Introduction:
In this chapter, we delve into the importance of individual action in addressing climate change and explore various ways individuals can contribute to the battle against climate change. While collective efforts and policy changes are crucial, empowering individuals to make sustainable choices in their daily lives can have a significant impact on reducing greenhouse gas emissions, promoting sustainable practices, and creating a more resilient future.

1. Sustainable Lifestyle Choices:
Individuals can make a difference by adopting sustainable lifestyle choices. This includes reducing energy consumption by using energy-efficient appliances, conserving water, minimizing waste generation through recycling and composting, and opting for sustainable modes of transportation like cycling or using public transit. By making conscious choices, individuals can contribute to reducing carbon footprints and mitigating climate change.

2. Renewable Energy Adoption:
Switching to renewable energy sources, such as solar or wind

power, at the individual level can have a substantial impact on reducing greenhouse gas emissions. Installing solar panels on rooftops or participating in community solar projects allows individuals to generate clean energy and contribute to the transition to a low-carbon future.

3. Consumer Choices:
Individuals can support sustainable practices by making environmentally conscious consumer choices. This includes purchasing products with minimal packaging, opting for locally sourced and organic food, and supporting companies that prioritize sustainability and social responsibility. By demanding sustainable products, individuals can influence market trends and encourage businesses to adopt more sustainable practices.

4. Advocacy and Education:
Empowering individuals to become advocates for climate action is crucial. By sharing knowledge, engaging in discussions, and raising awareness about climate change and its impacts, individuals can inspire others to take action. This can be done through personal networks, community events, social media, or joining environmental organizations. Education and information play a vital role in mobilizing individuals and fostering a sense of collective responsibility.

Real-Life Examples:
The "Fridays for Future" movement, initiated by young climate activist Greta Thunberg, has empowered millions of individuals worldwide to join climate strikes and demand policy changes. The "Zero Waste" movement encourages individuals to reduce waste and embrace a more sustainable lifestyle by adopting practices like bulk shopping, composting, and avoiding single-use plastics. Online platforms such as "Carbon Footprint Calculators" help individuals assess their carbon footprints and provide recommendations for reducing emissions.

Conclusion:

Individual action plays a crucial role in combating climate change. By making sustainable lifestyle choices, adopting renewable energy, making informed consumer decisions, and advocating for climate action, individuals can contribute to a collective effort to address the climate crisis. Small actions, when multiplied by millions, can create significant positive change. Empowering individuals to take action and providing them with the tools and knowledge to make sustainable choices are essential steps towards building a more sustainable and resilient future.

CHAPTER 28:
ART, MEDIA, AND COMMUNICATION FOR CLIMATE AWARENESS

Introduction:
In this chapter, we explore the power of art, media, and communication in raising awareness about climate change and inspiring action. Through various forms of artistic expression and effective communication strategies, artists, journalists, filmmakers, and activists play a crucial role in bringing the urgent message of climate change to a wider audience. We examine how art and media can convey the complex challenges of climate change, evoke emotional responses, and catalyse positive change.

1. Art as a Catalyst for Change:
Art can transcend language and convey messages in a compelling and emotive way. Artists from various disciplines use their creative expressions to raise awareness about climate change. For example, environmental installations, sculptures, and murals can engage communities, provoke thought, and spark conversations about the impacts of climate change. Artists often collaborate with scientists and activists to amplify their message and bring attention to critical environmental issues.

2. Documentary Films and Climate Change:
Documentary films have proven to be powerful tools for

educating and inspiring audiences about climate change. Documentaries like "An Inconvenient Truth" and "Chasing Ice" have captured the attention of millions, presenting scientific evidence, personal stories, and real-life examples of climate change impacts. These films not only inform but also motivate viewers to take action, showcasing solutions and inspiring individuals to make a difference.

3. Journalism and Climate Reporting:
Journalists and media organizations play a crucial role in shaping public opinion and influencing policy discussions around climate change. Investigative reporting, data-driven journalism, and in-depth analysis help uncover the complexities of climate change, expose environmental injustices, and hold governments and corporations accountable. Climate journalists also cover stories of resilience and innovative solutions, inspiring individuals, and communities to take action.

4. social media and Climate Activism:
Social media platforms provide a powerful and accessible means of communication for climate activists and organizations. Hashtags like #ClimateAction, #FridaysForFuture, and #ClimateStrike have mobilized millions of individuals worldwide to engage in online activism and offline demonstrations. Social media platforms enable the sharing of information, personal stories, and calls to action, amplifying the reach and impact of climate campaigns.

Real-Life Examples:
Art installations like Olafur Eliasson's "Ice Watch" brought chunks of melting ice from Greenland to city centres, visually demonstrating the urgency of melting ice caps due to climate change. The documentary film "Before the Flood" featuring Leonardo DiCaprio explores the global impacts of climate change, sparking conversations and inspiring viewers to take action. Environmental journalists like Naomi Klein and Bill McKibben have used their platforms to raise awareness about climate

change and advocate for policy changes. Greta Thunberg's use of social media has galvanized a global youth movement, inspiring millions to demand climate action.

Conclusion:

Art, media, and communication play vital roles in raising awareness about climate change, engaging communities, and inspiring action. Through their creative expressions, documentaries, journalism, and social media activism, artists, journalists, and climate communicators contribute to the global movement for climate action. By evoking emotional responses, presenting scientific evidence, and highlighting stories of resilience and solutions, they empower individuals to become advocates for change and drive collective action to address the climate crisis. Art, media, and communication have the power to shape public discourse and inspire a sustainable and resilient future.

PART VIII: LOOKING AHEAD

CHAPTER 29:
THE ROLE OF TECHNOLOGY IN CLIMATE MITIGATION

Introduction:
In this chapter, we delve into the significant role that technology plays in mitigating climate change. From renewable energy and energy-efficient solutions to carbon capture and storage, technological advancements offer promising opportunities for reducing greenhouse gas emissions and transitioning to a more sustainable future. We explore various technologies and their real-world applications, highlighting their potential to address the challenges of climate change.

1. Renewable Energy:
Renewable energy sources such as solar, wind, hydro, and geothermal power are key components of the transition to a low-carbon economy. The falling costs and increasing efficiency of renewable energy technologies have led to their widespread adoption. Real-life examples include the rapid growth of solar power installations in countries like China and India, the expansion of wind farms in Europe and the United States, and the use of hydroelectric power in countries like Norway and Brazil. These technologies offer clean and abundant sources of energy that can replace fossil fuels and contribute to substantial

emissions reductions.

2. Energy Efficiency:
Improving energy efficiency is another crucial aspect of climate mitigation. Energy-efficient technologies and practices help reduce energy consumption, resulting in lower greenhouse gas emissions. Examples of energy-efficient technologies include smart thermostats, LED lighting, and energy-efficient appliances. Real-life examples include the retrofitting of buildings with energy-saving measures, the implementation of energy management systems in industries, and the adoption of energy-efficient transportation options such as electric vehicles.

3. Carbon Capture and Storage (CCS):
Carbon capture and storage technologies aim to capture carbon dioxide emissions from industrial processes and power plants and store them underground. This approach can significantly reduce emissions from large-scale sources. Real-life examples include the use of CCS in the Sleipner gas field in Norway and the Boundary Dam coal-fired power plant in Canada. These projects demonstrate the potential of CCS to mitigate emissions from fossil fuel-intensive industries.

4. Sustainable Agriculture and Land Use:
Technology also plays a crucial role in addressing emissions from agriculture and land use. Precision agriculture techniques, including the use of sensors and data analytics, help optimize farming practices, reduce resource inputs, and minimize greenhouse gas emissions. Additionally, advances in remote sensing and satellite imagery assist in monitoring deforestation, land degradation, and land-use changes. These technologies enable more sustainable land management practices, such as reforestation and restoration efforts.

Real-Life Examples:
The Ivanpah Solar Power Facility in the Mojave Desert, California, is one of the world's largest solar thermal power

plants, generating clean energy to power hundreds of thousands of homes. Tesla's Gigafactory in Nevada produces lithium-ion batteries at a large scale, supporting the expansion of electric vehicles and renewable energy storage. The deployment of offshore wind farms, such as the London Array in the UK, showcases the potential of wind energy in supplying clean electricity to coastal communities. The Great Green Wall initiative in Africa uses technology and nature-based solutions to combat desertification and improve land resilience.

Conclusion:
Technology plays a vital role in climate mitigation by enabling the transition to renewable energy, improving energy efficiency, capturing, and storing carbon emissions, and promoting sustainable land use and agriculture. Real-life examples demonstrate the successful implementation of these technologies and their potential to reduce greenhouse gas emissions. However, it is essential to recognize that technology alone cannot solve the climate crisis. Effective policies, investment in research and development, and global cooperation are necessary to maximize the impact of technology in mitigating climate change. By harnessing the power of technology, we can accelerate the transition to a low-carbon economy and create a more sustainable and resilient future.

CHAPTER 30: LONG-TERM STRATEGIES FOR A RESILIENT FUTURE

Introduction:

In this chapter, we explore the importance of long-term strategies in building a resilient future in the face of climate change. As the impacts of climate change continue to manifest, it is crucial to develop comprehensive and adaptive approaches that can withstand and mitigate these challenges. We delve into the key elements of long-term strategies and examine real-life examples of successful initiatives that prioritize resilience and sustainability.

1. Integrated Planning and Policy Frameworks:

Long-term strategies for resilience require the integration of climate considerations into planning and policy frameworks. Governments at various levels need to develop robust adaptation and mitigation plans that consider the specific vulnerabilities and risks of their regions. These plans should encompass multiple sectors, including infrastructure, agriculture, water resources, and public health. Real-life examples include the Climate Action Plans implemented by cities like Copenhagen, Denmark, and Stockholm, Sweden, which incorporate comprehensive measures to reduce emissions and build resilience.

2. Nature-Based Solutions:

Nature-based solutions involve utilizing and restoring natural ecosystems to enhance resilience and mitigate climate impacts. Examples include reforestation efforts, the creation of green spaces, and the restoration of wetlands and coastal habitats. These solutions not only help sequester carbon but also provide multiple co-benefits, such as flood mitigation, biodiversity conservation, and improved air and water quality. Real-life examples include the restoration of the Great Barrier Reef in Australia and the implementation of green infrastructure projects in cities like New York City, which use natural features to manage stormwater and reduce the urban heat island effect.

3. Building Resilient Infrastructure:
Infrastructure plays a critical role in determining a community's ability to withstand and recover from climate-related events. Long-term strategies for resilience involve designing and retrofitting infrastructure to be climate-resilient and adaptable. This includes considering sea-level rise, extreme weather events, and changing precipitation patterns in infrastructure planning and design. Real-life examples include the Netherlands' Delta Works, a system of dams and barriers that protect against rising sea levels, and the design of sustainable and resilient buildings and transportation systems in cities like Singapore.

4. Community Engagement and Social Equity:
Long-term strategies for resilience should prioritize community engagement and social equity to ensure that the most vulnerable populations are not disproportionately affected by climate change. This involves including marginalized communities in decision-making processes, providing access to information and resources, and addressing social and economic disparities. Real-life examples include community-led climate action initiatives, such as the Resilient Puerto Rico Advisory Commission, which aims to empower local communities in building resilience after the devastating impacts of Hurricane Maria.

Conclusion:
Long-term strategies for a resilient future are essential

for adapting to and mitigating the impacts of climate change. Integrated planning, nature-based solutions, resilient infrastructure, and community engagement are key elements of these strategies. Real-life examples demonstrate the successful implementation of these approaches in various contexts, highlighting the importance of proactive and adaptive measures. By embracing long-term strategies and prioritizing resilience, communities and societies can build a sustainable and resilient future that can withstand the challenges of a changing climate.

32. Chapter 32: Education and Climate Literacy

CHAPTER 32: EDUCATION AND CLIMATE LITERACY

Introduction:
Education plays a vital role in addressing the climate crisis by empowering individuals with the knowledge, skills, and attitudes necessary to understand and take action on climate change. In this chapter, we explore the importance of climate literacy and the role of education in fostering a sustainable and resilient future. We delve into the key components of climate education, highlight real-life examples of effective initiatives, and discuss the transformative power of education in building a more sustainable world.

1. Climate Literacy:
Climate literacy refers to the understanding of climate science, the impacts of climate change, and the solutions needed to mitigate and adapt to its effects. It involves developing knowledge about the Earth's climate system, greenhouse gas emissions, and the link between human activities and climate change. Climate literacy also includes an understanding of the social, economic, and environmental dimensions of the climate crisis. By promoting climate literacy, education equips individuals with the knowledge necessary to make informed decisions and take meaningful action.

2. Integrating Climate Education:

Climate education can be integrated into various educational settings, including schools, universities, and informal learning environments. It can be incorporated across disciplines, such as science, social studies, geography, and ethics, to provide a comprehensive understanding of the climate crisis. Real-life examples include the Climate Change Schools Program in the United Kingdom, which integrates climate change topics into the curriculum across multiple subjects, and the Eco-Schools program, which encourages students to take action on sustainability issues.

3. Experiential Learning and Field Studies:
Experiential learning and field studies provide hands-on opportunities for students to engage with the natural environment and witness the impacts of climate change first-hand. Field trips to environmentally significant areas, participation in citizen science projects, and engaging in outdoor learning activities help deepen students' understanding of climate change and foster a connection with nature. Real-life examples include the Climate Stewards Program in the United States, where students participate in ecological restoration projects, and the Youth Climate Summits that bring together young people to learn and collaborate on climate solutions.

4. Climate Justice and Equity in Education:
Climate education should prioritize promoting climate justice and equity by ensuring that all individuals, regardless of background or socio-economic status, have access to climate education opportunities. It is essential to address the disproportionate impacts of climate change on marginalized communities and empower students to become agents of change in their communities. Real-life examples include the Environmental and Climate Justice Education Project in South Africa, which focuses on engaging communities in climate education and promoting environmental justice.

5. Education for Sustainable Development:

Education for sustainable development emphasizes the integration of environmental, social, and economic dimensions of sustainability into the educational system. It encourages critical thinking, problem-solving, and active citizenship, empowering individuals to contribute to sustainable practices and advocate for climate action. Real-life examples include the Green Schools Initiative, which promotes sustainability practices in schools, and the Earth Charter Initiative, which provides a framework for ethical and sustainable decision-making.

Conclusion:
Education and climate literacy are powerful tools in addressing the climate crisis. By equipping individuals with the knowledge, skills, and attitudes needed to understand and take action on climate change, education plays a crucial role in building a sustainable and resilient future. Integrating climate education, promoting experiential learning, addressing climate justice, and emphasizing sustainable development are key components of effective climate education initiatives. Through education, we can empower individuals to become informed global citizens and drive the transformative changes necessary to combat climate change.

PART IX: CONCLUSION

CHAPTER 33: LESSONS LEARNED AND THE PATH FORWARD

Introduction:
In this final chapter, we reflect on the lessons learned from our journey through the climate crisis and explore the path forward towards a sustainable and resilient future. We examine the key takeaways from the previous chapters, discuss the challenges that lie ahead, and highlight the opportunities for collective action and positive change. By learning from both the successes and failures of the past, we can shape a better future for ourselves and future generations.

1. Lessons from Success Stories:
Throughout this book, we have encountered numerous success stories and real-life examples of individuals, communities, organizations, and governments taking action to address the climate crisis. From renewable energy initiatives to sustainable agriculture practices, these success stories demonstrate the effectiveness of collective efforts in mitigating and adapting to climate change. By analysing these examples, we can identify common strategies, best practices, and innovative approaches that can be replicated and scaled up.

2. The Power of Collaboration:
One of the most significant lessons learned is the power of collaboration and partnerships in tackling the climate crisis.

The successful initiatives we have explored have often involved diverse stakeholders working together towards a common goal. Collaboration between governments, businesses, civil society organizations, and local communities has led to the development and implementation of effective climate solutions. Examples include the Paris Agreement, a global collaboration among nations to combat climate change, and the We Are Still In coalition, where U.S. states, cities, and businesses work together to uphold climate commitments.

3. Overcoming Challenges:
Addressing the climate crisis is not without challenges. We have witnessed obstacles such as political resistance, economic barriers, and social inertia. However, the lessons learned from past experiences teach us that perseverance, innovation, and advocacy are crucial in overcoming these challenges. The fossil fuel divestment movement, which encourages institutions to withdraw investments from the fossil fuel industry, is an example of how collective action can push for change despite powerful interests.

4. Empowering Individuals:
Individuals have a significant role to play in driving climate action. The chapters in this book have highlighted the importance of individual choices, consumer behaviour, and grassroots movements. By adopting sustainable lifestyles, advocating for change, and demanding climate action from policymakers and businesses, individuals can contribute to the collective effort in combating climate change. The Fridays for Future movement, led by young climate activist Greta Thunberg, demonstrates the power of individual voices in raising awareness and demanding urgent climate action.

5. The Path Forward:
Moving forward, it is crucial to build upon the lessons learned and take decisive action to address the climate crisis. This includes transitioning to renewable energy sources, implementing

sustainable land and water management practices, promoting green technologies and innovation, investing in climate-resilient infrastructure, and prioritizing social and environmental justice. Policies and regulations that support climate action must be enacted at local, national, and international levels. Collaborative efforts and partnerships should be strengthened to ensure a coordinated response to the climate crisis.

Conclusion:

As we conclude our exploration of the climate crisis, it is clear that we are at a critical juncture in human history. The lessons learned from the successes and challenges of the past provide a roadmap for the future. By harnessing the power of collaboration, empowering individuals, and learning from real-life examples, we can forge a path towards a sustainable and resilient future. The urgency of the climate crisis demands bold and decisive action from all sectors of society. Let us draw inspiration from the lessons learned and work together to create a world that is safer, healthier, and more sustainable for generations to come.